Pie Corbett's Reading Spine

The best books to share with your class!

" Imagine a primary school where, over seven or eight years, children are read to, enjoy, discuss and work with a core of around 80 books. These 'essential reads' would be a store of classics, creating a living library inside a child's mind. This is the 'reading spine'. Schools that have a reading spine build a common bank of stories that bind the community together. These are shared and deeply imagined common experiences. "

Pie Corbett

■ SCHOLASTIC

Book End, Range Road, Witney, Oxfordshire, OX29 0YD
www.scholastic.co.uk
© 2015, Scholastic Ltd

456789 890123

British Library Cataloguing-in-Publication Data
A catalogue record for this book is available from the British Library.

ISBN 978-1407-12896-2
Printed by Ashford Colour Press

Editorial
Robin Hunt

Design
Scholastic Design Team: Neil Salt, Nicolle Thomas

Cover Design
Neil Salt

Contents

Where's Spot?
Dear Zoo
You Choose
We're Going On a Bear Hunt
Brown Bear, Brown Bear, What Do You See?
Jasper's Beanstalk
The Very Hungry Caterpillar
Hairy Maclary from Donaldson's Dairy
Each Peach Pear Plum
Hug
The Train Ride
Come On Daisy

Owl Babies
The Gruffalo
Handa's Surprise
Mr Gumpy's Outing
Rosie's Walk
Six Dinner Sid
Mrs Armitage
Whatever Next
On the Way Home
Farmer Duck
Goodnight Moon
Shhh!

Peace at Last
Can't You Sleep Little Bear?
Where the Wild Things Are
The Elephant and the Bad Baby
Avocado Baby
The Tiger Who Came to Tea
Lost and Found
Knuffle Bunny
Beegu
Dogger
Cops and Robbers
Elmer

Contents

INTRODUCTION

Pie Corbett's
Reading Spine

Imagine a primary school where over 7 or 8 years, children are read to, enjoy, discuss and work with around 82 core books. These 'essential reads' would be a store of classics, creating a living library inside a child's mind. This is the 'Reading Spine'.

Great Books

Great books build the imagination. The more we read aloud expressively, and the more children are able to savour, discuss and reinterpret literature through the arts, the more memorable the characters, places and events become, building an inner world. A child who is read to will have an inner kingdom of unicorns, talking spiders and a knife that cuts into other worlds. The mind is like a 'tardis'; it may seem small but inside there are many mansions. Each great book develops the imagination and equips the reader with language.

Great Stories

Great stories speak to us as individuals and some children will return to certain books again and again. Great stories also build our language because around 75 per cent of our vocabulary comes from our reading. Reading develops the ability to think in the abstract; to follow lines of thought. Schools that have a reading spine, build a common bank of stories that bind the community together. These are shared and deeply imagined common experiences.

What is the Reading Spine?

The Reading Spine should be central to every school's book stock, but should also be supplemented by many other books. In the Foundation Stage and Year 1, I have suggested a spine of 12 great picture books with which children should build a strong acquaintance.

Year 2 is a transition year, with both great picture books and 'chapter stories' included. The daily read-aloud programme is supplemented by guided, shared and independent reading.

In the Reading Spine at Key Stage 2, I have selected six novels in each year with a focus on one core picture book. This leaves enough space for teachers to add their own enthusiasms and new finds.

❝ A child who is read to will have an inner kingdom of unicorns, talking spiders and a knife that cuts into other worlds. ❞

Pie Corbett

Steps to a
Reading Spine

STEP 1

Establish the core of key books that all children will experience: these should be 'must have' reads – the classics. The finest books that you can find! Leave space to add other books that come along or might suit the class. The aim is for every child to experience the pleasure and challenge of great literature.

STEP 2

Resource the core list: class sets are very useful so that the books can then be used for close study. As well as this, sets of six books can be used for guided reading. Also, try to gather other books/films by the same author for a wider author study.

STEP 3

On a daily basis develop your ability to read aloud for pleasure with expression on a daily basis, bringing the story alive for children.

STEP 4

Help children to inhabit the world of the story through book discussion, drama, art, dance, music, writing-in-role and play. Imaginative engagement with the text draws children into the tale, and makes it a deeper, more memorable and meaningful experience.

STEP 5

Learn how to draw on the core books to teach writing, for example, if you are teaching dialogue, use the core books as exemplars. In this way, both you and the children are constantly drawing on quality models that they will begin to know well. Moreover, the books will help to develop and deepen the children's imaginative world, as well as becoming a key resource for their writing.

STEP 6

You will also need to thread in poetry. *The Works Key Stage 1* (which includes Reception) and *The Works Key Stage 2* (both Macmillan Children's Books) provide banks of poems for enjoying, performing and discussing, and some may be used as models for writing. At the back of these two anthologies, the poems are organised by year group to create a poetry spine. You may also wish to select core poets for each term. Finally, it is important to thread into the Reading Spine high quality non-fiction. These books could be selected in relation to topics being studied, but there may also be key books that a school wishes to ensure children have encountered, such as *The Diary of Anne Frank*.

❝ Establish the core of key books that all children will experience: these should be 'must have' reads – the classics. The finest books that you can find! ❞

Top tips for using
picture books (1)

Of course, any teacher could come up with an activity linked to a book. The key is to think about activities that will illuminate the meaning, help children engage at a deeper level and enter the world of the story. Here is a whole alphabet of activities that should spark your children's imagination:

A Show the front/back cover. Ask: *What sort of story is this? What might happen? Tell the story to a partner based on the cover image or start from the title.*

B Read through and pause every so often. Ask: *What is going to happen next? Write, tell or draw the next page, then discuss.*

C Invite the children to discuss what they enjoyed about the book or what it reminded them of or meant to them.

D Explore links and connections. Ask: *Can you find where the story repeats itself? Are there links between this story and our lives, or between this story and other stories?*

E As a class list possible questions, such as things we are not sure about and would like to discuss. List the questions and then choose the ones that would be most fruitful to talk about.

F Role-play a scene immediately after the book has finished or before the story starts. Alternatively, select an image from the middle of the book. Ask: *What is happening? What might happen immediately before and after?*

G Ask children to draw a map of the story and retell in their own words. Change the nature of a character or alter a key event.

H Cover the dialogue with a sticky note before inviting the children to draw a speech bubble and to write, then dramatise the conversation.

I Pause the reading and 'freeze-frame' the page, then interview each character that appears on it. Ask: *What are you thinking/feeling/hoping will happen next? What are you regretting?* Alternatively, use thought bubbles to explore the above.

J Initiate a group performance using expression.

K Use 'what if' statements to raise different possibilities in the narrative.

L Re-enact the story by creating a whole-class physical map, using children to represent parts of the story. Then interview bystanders or even objects in role as observers of the story – what did they see happen?

❝ The key is to think about activities that will illuminate the meaning, help children engage at a deeper level and enter the world of the story. ❞

Top tips for using
picture books (2)

M Use percussive instruments and ask children to work in groups to set the story to simple rhythms and musical patterns.

N With the whole class create a dance to accompany a story, such as the 'rumpus' in *Where the Wild Things Are* (HarperCollins).

O Invite the children to illustrate or create a wall map (using lining paper). Use print-making or patterning to accompany a tale, picking up on an aspect in the story or images.

P Let the children choose how they will respond to a text – and add to your own repertoire of possibilities from their ideas.

Q Use a shoebox to create a diorama of a key scene.

R Fill a story bag with objects or puppets and a map linked to a story, so that children can take the book home and explore the story through play.

S Retell the story in small groups with some children playing a role and others providing the narrator's voice.

T Display selected images and ask them if they can work out what might happen on the pages before and after. Alternatively, each group is given a picture and develops a telling of the story for that page as they see it. Then, the whole class performs their section of the story in order to see how well the story flows. Another option is to show three images from different parts of the story. Ask: *In which order should the images be placed – and why?*

U In role as a character, encourage children to step out of the tale and interact in a different environment or scene. For example, join in with 'tea-time' at the three bears' cottage.

V On the first reading use sticky notes to cover key words in a story. Let the children discuss what they think the words might be, or what the effect on the reader will be for their choice.

W Rewrite a page but add extra description to compensate for withdrawing a picture. With the class compare the original page with the rewritten page.

X Show the class just the pictures in the story. Can the children tell the story using only the images?

Y With the children make a 3D model of something from a story, such as objects or settings.

Z Provide costumes or hats for the children to use in a role play.

Top tips for using novels (1)

Decide on where you will stop reading in order to carry out each activity or discussion. Here is a whole alphabet of activities that should spark your children's imagination.

A Ask the children to discuss their preferences and to explain their ideas.

B Together explore links and connections. Ask: *Are there links between this story, other stories or works of art? How does the tale make a link with your own life?*

C Ask the children to list possible questions, such as things that they are not sure about and would be useful to discuss. List the questions and then choose the ones that would be most fruitful to talk about.

D In pairs, encourage gossip about the events so far.

E In stories where the characters have problems to solve, invite children to work in pairs with one in role as an agony aunt and the other in role as a character who will explain the problem. Encourage the 'agony aunt' to provide some advice.

F In pairs, sit the children back to back with one child in role as a character phoning a friend. Encourage the character to explain what has been going on while the friend listens and then responds with advice.

G Working in-role as a character, invite the children to write a diary entry or letter to a friend about the main event/what has just happened. Alternatively, they could write to a character offering advice.

H In role as journalists, invite the children to interview a character and write a news item – or broadcast it, with an 'outside broadcasting unit' carrying out the interview.

I With the class create and film a cartoon or filmed version of the scene.

J Build a story museum with the children to represent scenes from the novel by gathering and displaying objects, sounds (use talking tins) and images from the story.

K Provide or create with the children news bulletins for key moments in the story.

L Together draw 'feelings graphs' showing the ups and down for the different characters in the story.

❝ Here is a whole alphabet of activities that should spark your children's imagination. ❞

Top tips for using novels (2)

M Encourage children to choose their favourite word, phrase, line or section and share. Ask: *Why do you like that part?*

N Display images and ask: *Which is the one image that says the most in the story? What does it say to the reader?*

O With the class select words that encapsulate the essence of the book. Make a list of these key words and then select the 'best'/'truest' five words.

P Let them choose a favourite line, phrase or word from the novel. Invite them to stand in a circle, take it in turns to step into the circle and say the word aloud with a gesture. Encourage everyone else to then repeat the word and gesture.

Q Stand the group in a circle and ask each of them to choose an action from an event in the story that is memorable, then step into the circle and mime the action. Then everyone else can imitate the action.

R In pairs, encourage them to retell the story word-by-word or sentence-by-sentence, or retell the story in cartoon form.

S As a whole class select all the verbs from an action passage and list them in the order that they appear. Can they say them aloud with expression? Ask: *What is the effect?* Now try the same thing with the adjectives or nouns.

T Provide time for individuals to create items from a book, including letters, diary entries, news items, postcards – any written item that appears in a story or might appear.

U Invite children to role-play any event in a story that takes place in a different setting, but is referred to or suggested by the book.

V During a reading session with the class alter a story by stopping, considering possible plot lines and then retelling the story or rewriting it.

W As a whole class put especially bad characters on trial.

X Ask children to create the back page blurb for the story and design a new cover or advert.

Y Invite groups to create a 'for sale' advert for a character or the book itself.

Z Provide time for children to write an end-of-term report for a character.

Reading and
sharing the books (1)

Read from the class novel or picture book on a daily basis. It is worth taking the time to read the books through beforehand and thinking about where you might wish to stop for discussion or some sort of activity. Anyone can dream up 50 things to do with a book, but the key is to halt at moments where an activity or discussion is needed to deepen engagement and understanding.

On most occasions, picture books should be read straight through without endlessly stopping – the children want to hear the story! Only occasionally might there be a moment to pause where a situation has been set up and it is worth asking the children to think about the possibilities for what might happen next. However, a good picture book will demand re-reading over a number of days so that you can focus on different aspects of the story.

'Talk for Reading' is a form of comprehension that can be carried out with the class or with a small group. It involves an open discussion about a worthwhile text, intending to develop engagement and the ability to read critically, deepening understanding and therefore appreciation. This form of talk is highlighted constantly in the new National Curriculum in England and should take place often. The skill is for the teacher to become a *good listener*, prompting the children to do most of the wondering, thinking, exploring, suggesting and summarising.

The principles of 'Talk for Reading'

- All ideas are accepted and given serious consideration.
- Everyone should think, try and 'have a go' at contributing.
- You can build on someone else's ideas.
- You can also challenge someone's ideas by putting forward alternative thoughts.

- Be ready to change your mind.
- Everyone must listen to each other.

The teacher's role is to instigate a conversation, acting as an interested listener and occasionally holding up an idea for further inspection by repeating what has been said. The teacher may also draw attention to certain sections of a book that might benefit from further thinking by focusing the children. The children are trained to read sentence-by-sentence (or image-by-image) from the beginning all the way through, tying ideas together as they go along, revising their thinking in the light of new information and making connections across a text. Much of the talk will hinge around what intrigues us as readers, constantly raising questions and putting forward possible interpretations. Make a list of tentative phrases that might help children talk, for example: *I'm not sure but... We wondered whether .... The writer seems to be suggesting that...*

Over time, the children move to a stage where they carry out almost all of the talking – often interpreting at length and talking through their understanding aloud. At first, this may have to be modelled by the teacher, but very soon the children will latch on to the idea. It is important though that the teacher does not dominate the thinking and talking.

> **❝ On most occasions, picture books should be read straight through without endlessly stopping – the children want to hear the story! ❞**

Reading and
sharing the books (2)

Things to talk about might include:

- initial ideas, thoughts, feelings, memories, experiences, possibilities and questions;
- what did we imagine, think and feel;
- what might have happened before the passage;
- what might happen next – predicting and clarifying;
- statements about what the words mean – commenting, referring to the textual evidence;
- vocabulary – other words that might have been used;
- key words that provoke interest;
- how the writing is hooking the reader;
- inferences/deductions – work out from the clues in the text;
- possible meanings;
- re-reading constantly for fluency – to emphasise meaning;
- saying a sentence aloud using expression – discussing possible different ways of 'saying' the sentence, noticing punctuation;
- changing an idea in the light of new information/ events;
- seeing events from the different viewpoints of characters/sides of an argument;
- visualising – what you can see inside your head;
- reading the pictures, thinking about the effect of the image on the reader and considering the contrast between the words and the images;
- raising questions – wondering;
- making connections with our own experiences or making connections between books;
- reading as a writer – discussing organisation, sentence patterns, word choice in relation to effect – the writing style;
- drawing the threads together – summarising;
- discussing the overarching theme or line of argument – evaluation and personal preferences.

It is important that the children do not have to play 'guess what is in teacher's head'. The teacher is interested in developing the children's thinking, though it is worth remembering that the teacher is not the sole provider of wisdom. Through gradual scaffolding and building on each other's thoughts, as well as challenging, we can discuss collectively and co-construct new thinking, deepening understanding. When this is done well, the teacher will find their own understanding deepened with new insights gathered from the children. The teacher's role is to listen, to reflect, to focus attention and to help children deepen engagement and understanding.

As the Reading Spine has been carefully selected, you will find that there are links between the themes and concerns of many of the stories. *In which ways are they alike or different?* It is this sort of talk that should become a byword for working with the Reading Spine. These are intriguing, deep and challenging books. There will be much to discuss. This should become a habit so that children constantly get the most out of quality literature and think deeply, carefully and cautiously to illuminate their thinking. This should constitute every child's experience of reading.

Please note: for each year group the books have been set out in the order in which they might be read, as the final books in each section tend to be more demanding. Always read the books first to decide if they are appropriate. Read Aidan Chamber's book *Tell Me* (Thimble Press) for more about oral comprehension.

❝ The teacher's role is to listen, to reflect, to focus attention and to help children deepen engagement and understanding. ❞

Pie Corbett's
Reading Spine

The books that I have chosen are almost all very repetitive and rather like songs!
This makes them easier for children to join in with so that the experience of reading
becomes interactive and the children begin to learn the story as they are read to.
In each book there will be much to discuss so that the children understand the
vocabulary as well as what is happening.

All of the books have pictures, which support the text but also compliment and add to it.
It is important to discuss the pictures and what is happening in them as much as the text.
After a while, the children will get to know each story word for word, which can give great
confidence to early readers in terms of fluency when reading.

Where's Spot?

Eric Hill (Puffin)

Both this book and *Dear Zoo* work on the same principle of
involving the child in the act of reading by using flaps so that the
process becomes interactive. Both books can be used to create
new versions by hiding a different animal under homemade flaps.
Use the game of 'hide and seek' when playing.

Dear Zoo

Rod Campbell (Puffin)

This book is a gateway into learning about different animals. The repetition
of '*so*' will add a new conjunction to a child's repertoire. Discuss the reasons
for sending the animals back – *heavy, fragile, tall, dangerous, fierce, grumpy,*
'*with care*', *scary, naughty, jumpy* and *perfect*. Use masks or toys or puppets
and involve the children in the story, playing different parts.

You Choose

Pippa Goodhart and Nick Sharratt (Random House)

This classic book is good to share many times, especially working closely
with a few children so they can look at the pictures and choose. Invite
children to make collections – organising toys or objects into different
categories. Play sorting games – by size, colour, shape or type. Use the
book many times to choose a main character, a setting, an animal or
object. Use these selections then to make up simple stories. The book
can be used endlessly for this as the combinations are almost infinite!.

We're Going on a Bear Hunt READ&RESPOND

Michael Rosen (Walker Books)

Learn the story orally, map it and act it out outside. Ask: *Why does the writer say 'we're not scared' at the very start of the story? Who is scared?* Talk about how everyone feels at different points. Ask: *Was the bear angry or did he just want a friend?* Look at the different places and invent other onomatopoeic phrases (*swishy swashy*). Draw a new map, perhaps of the local area, and create a new version. Act or sing the new version, with costumes or puppets and film it for parents. (See the *Read & Respond* title for further ideas.)

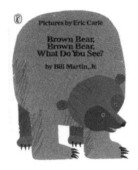

Brown Bear, Brown Bear, What Do You See?

Bill Martin Jnr and Eric Carle (Windmill Books)

Read, enjoy and let children join in until they know the story. Leave copies around so they can 'play at reading'. Discuss what else the animals might hear, touch, taste or see. Ask: *How do the different colours make you feel? Which is your favourite?* Create a different version of the story for other animals that the children know, such as a cat or dog. Create tissue collages using primary colours or bold paintings of animals. Also, read *Polar Bear, Polar Bear, What Do You Hear?* by the same authors.

Jasper's Beanstalk READ&RESPOND

Nick Butterworth and Mick Inkpen (Hodder)

This story makes a neat precursor to *The Very Hungry Caterpillar* as it shows how to make up a simple story by repeating the days of the week and describing what happens on each day. Ask: *Who is Jasper and what is a beanstalk?* Read this in the Spring when you can grow some beanstalks – and tell the children the slightly scary story of 'Jack and the Beanstalk'. Discuss what happens at the end of this story – and then decide with the children what happens to Jasper at the top of the beanstalk!

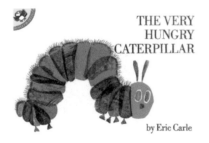

The Very Hungry Caterpillar

Eric Carle (Puffin)

Share until the children know the story well. Ask: *Who is 'Christa'?* Discuss the idea of the author/artist making the book for someone else. Create collages of the moon at night, leaves and trees. Notice the alliteration (*light/ little/ lay/ leaf*) and the introduction of another conjunction '*but*'. Ideal for getting a sense of days of the week, different fruit (bring in a selection) and growing! Of course, some of this work might best be done in the spring/summer when you can hatch out butterflies or at least see some outside! Paint huge, vibrant butterflies.

Hairy Maclary from Donaldson's Dairy

Lynley Dodd (Puffin)

Read this story many times with everyone joining in and savouring the rhymes. Ask: *Which is the favourite dog? Who is the least favourite?* Try inventing other similes instead of '*as big as a horse*', for example, '*as big as a car*'! Collect and list rhyming words. Play games to hear which words rhyme and which do not. Talk about names that we give pets.

Each Peach Pear Plum   READ&RESPOND

Allan and Janet Ahlberg (Puffin)

Read together and look carefully at each picture. Tell the class the stories or rhymes behind each of the characters. Make sure that the story books are available for the children to look at. Chant the book together and try inventing a rhythmic clap as a chorus between each page. Provide puppets or costumes and objects from the stories for play. (See the *Read & Respond* title for further ideas.)

Hug

Jez Alborough (Walker Books)

In this book there are of course lots of the different animals to name, but it is also important to let the children tell you how the monkey and the other animals feel and what they might be thinking. Get some sticky notes in the shape of speech bubbles and add in what characters might say or think. Avoid the temptation to tell the children! Make masks and play at the story – use toys or puppets to re-enact. Try making up the whole story with the class, write this up and turn it into a Big Book. The theme of losing a mother also features in *Come on, Daisy!* and in the Reception book *Owl Babies*.

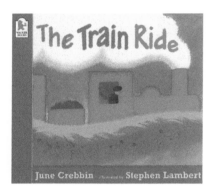

The Train Ride

June Crebbin (Walker Books)

Ideally, take the children on a train! If not, then use film and toys. Ask: *Who has been on a car or bus journey? Where did you go and what did you see? Who is the lady with the child? What is the town and what is the countryside?* There is plenty to discuss in the story – animals, meadows, hills, farms, tractors, tickets, tunnels, the seaside, lighthouse and sand. Ask: *Why are they travelling to Gran's?* Bring in a mirror so that everyone can see themselves. Make seaside small worlds using sand and water. Change the story and have a child coming from the country into the city and ask: *What would they see?* Lay out a train track.

Come on, Daisy!

Jane Simmons (Orchard Books)

Some children might have noticed by now the question marks in certain book titles and here we are now with an exclamation mark as well! Start with the cover. Ask: *Who is speaking, to whom and what might it mean? What do you think will happen in the story? Why must Daisy stay close?* Talk about: '*I'll try*'. Track Daisy's feelings. Emphasise the 'but' construction when reading with children joining in. Ask: *Are the dangers real? What is the book about? What is it telling us to do when we go out with Mum or Dad?*

Pie Corbett's
Reading Spine

The books for the 4–5 age group build on the Nursery selection. They still mainly use patterned language, but begin to have a stronger emotional connection with the reader. There is also plenty to discuss and to wonder about. Many of them lend themselves to retelling and creating new versions or further adventures featuring the same characters.

Owl Babies READ&RESPOND

Martin Waddell (Walker Books)

By now children should be familiar with the conventions of books such as cover, author, page-turning, as well as terms such as word, letter, full stops/capital letters, title, story and so on. Draw the distinction between the person who wrote the book and the artist. There is plenty for the children to discuss, especially the graded reactions of the three baby owls. Martin Waddell talks about getting the idea for the book from hearing a lost child in a supermarket crying, 'I want my Mummy'. This is a great book about basic feelings and comfort. Draw, paint or make huge owls. Make owl masks and act the story out as it is being told.

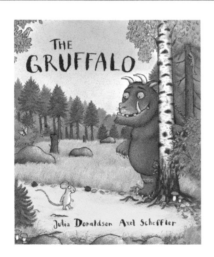

The Gruffalo

Julia Donaldson (Macmillan)

Everyone loves this book! Read and re-read it until the story is in the children's heart forever. Ask: *Why do the animals ask the mouse to come to their houses? Why does the mouse tell the animals about the Gruffalo? How is mouse really clever? Why is the Gruffalo 'bursting with laughter'?* Map the story to see the pattern and retell with plenty of actions. Use puppets/finger puppets to retell the tale. Make a Gruffalo den/corner. Paint an enormous Gruffalo picture.

Handa's Surprise READ&RESPOND

Eileen Browne (Walker Books)

This is another picture book, like *Rosie's Walk*, in which the pictures say more than the words. Make the effort to buy the fruit to show the children. Draw or paint the animals and fruit. Retell the story and act it out, using a wallpaper map. Change the animals and fruit to invent a new version. Discuss what we know about Kenya from the story. (See the *Read & Respond* titles for further ideas.)

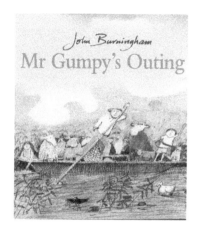

Mr Gumpy's Outing

John Burningham (Bloomsbury)

Another cumulative tale that can easily be used to make your own version. Ask: What happens when everyone comes 'for a ride another day'? Use a roll of sturdy lining paper and draw a long map. Use this to draw the different animals and write what they say inside speech bubbles. Ask: *Who in the story is naughty? Should Mr Gumpy have been more sensible?* This is a lovely story to chat about and play at. Provide the toy animals or puppets and a floor map.

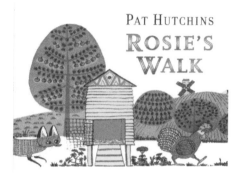

Rosie's Walk READ&RESPOND

Pat Hutchins (Random House)

This is a clever book. Try reading it to the children without looking at the pictures. Then show the book and enjoy the slapstick. Ask: *Is Rosie clever or is the fox silly?* Pick up on any design or pattern that interests the children and imitate with crayons or paints. Draw the map, notice the prepositions and create new journeys with a fierce animal following! (See *Read & Respond* title for further ideas.)

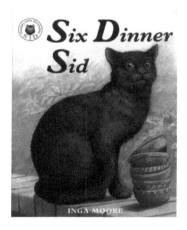

Six Dinner Sid

Inga Moore (Hodder)

It would be worth talking about pets and the vet before starting the story. Then read and enjoy the beautiful art work. Make the houses out of cardboard boxes and play at the story. Ask: *Why would the cat want six dinners? Why don't the neighbours talk to each other?* Discuss the six different characters and then invent new ones, using alliteration, such as: *As Clive he was curious…* Hold pretend phone calls between the vet and the owners about their cat, and then make up what the owners would say to each other about Sid! Ask: *How are the people in Pythagoras Street different and why was this better?*

Mrs Armitage

Quentin Blake (Random House)

Oh, the joy of Mrs Armitage! Make sure that you bring a real bike into the classroom! Read and all chant the story together. Discuss the pictures and words. Draw a huge basic bike and add extra ideas like Mrs Armitage. Recreate the bike in the classroom by starting with a chair and then add on all the things that are in the story. Finally, add sound effects and perform the story. Ask: *What might be added to the roller skates?*

Whatever Next READ&RESPOND

Jill Murphy (Macmillan)

Show the inside title page. Ask: *What sort of character will the bear be?* The story is an obvious invitation to wonder *'how could we make a rocket, where would we travel and who would we meet?'* Such play could lead to new versions of the story (*'You and your stories. Whatever next?'*). Ask: *Did Baby Bear really travel to the moon? Where did the story take place?* (See the *Read & Respond* title for further ideas.)

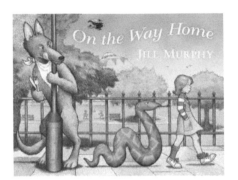

On the Way Home

Jill Murphy (Macmillan)

Look carefully at the front cover and ask: *What do we think is going to happen in the story?* Act the story out with children taking the different roles. Ask: *Why doesn't Claire tell the truth? Why does she cry at the end?* Notice how each mini story fits the basic story mountain pattern – main character, dilemma, resolution. With the class create your own versions, map, retell and write.

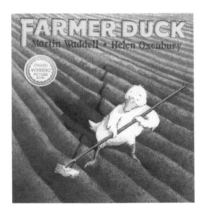

Farmer Duck

Martin Waddell (Walker Books)

This is basically Animal Farm for five-year-olds. Compare the inside cover spread at the front with the back – and the cover – what do they think is going to happen? Then look at the inner title page for more clues. Act out the animals meeting. Tell the story of what the farmer did next. Ask: *What did the animals say? Did they all set to work?* Set up a farm area for play. Write messages to the farmer!

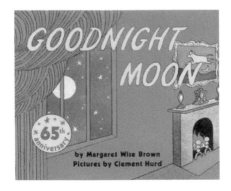

Goodnight Moon

Margaret Wise Brown (HarperCollins)

What other stories have a moon in them? (*Owl Babies, Where the Wild Things Are, Can't You Sleep Little Bear?*). Make a list of all the things in your classroom and say: *In the classroom there was a clock, chair, a sand tray, a computer and lots of tables.* Then say good night to all these things and extend each idea – present this as a list poem. For example: *Goodnight clock that ticks. Goodnight chair where we can sit. Goodnight sand tray where we play each day.* This is a gentle and comforting story for the end of the day. Let children take it in turns to read or tell the story in a role-play area to a baby – and NOT just the girls. Let them learn to be comfortable with a book at an early age.

SCHOLASTIC

Shhh!

Sally Grindley (Bloomsbury)

This amazing book is very good for sharing with parents, as the way the book is written demonstrates to parents how to read with their child. Read, join in and enjoy the story many times. Look for clues about what is on the next page and look carefully at each page as there is plenty to notice and comment upon. Think about how the characters feel. Tell the story of Jack and his visit to a giant's castle.

Pie Corbett's
Reading Spine

The picture books in Year 1 offer deeper exploration of emotions and wonder. They are mainly rooted in the everyday crises of life. Again, most of these books lend themselves to setting up a variety of play situations – using toys, costumes and puppets – but the children also need to be involved in careful reading of the books, paying close attention to the detail and entering imagined worlds to experience the stories deeply – then talking it all through.

Peace at Last
Jill Murphy (Macmillan)

Ask the children: *What is peace?* Make a list of peaceful times (*I am peaceful when…*). You might need to explain 'snore' before reading the book! Ask: *Why can Mr Bear not sleep?* Make a list of all the noises he can hear. Turn this into a list poem and add other ideas. For example: *At night, I hear the cats fighting outside. I can hear the buses driving by. I hear the kitchen tap dripping.*

Can't You Sleep Little Bear? `READ&RESPOND`
Martin Waddell (Walker Books)

Follow both bears and talk about what they feel or are thinking. Ask: *Is Little Bear really trying to go to sleep? How does Big Bear comfort Little Bear?* Re-read this book many times, as it is about comfort and feeling safe. (See the *Read & Respond* title for further ideas.)

Where the Wild Things Are
Maurice Sendak (HarperCollins)

Look at the cover. Ask: *What might happen? Who is creating mischief? What really happened in Max's room that night?* Create a 'Wild Things' dance – *'be still'* and then *'let the wild rumpus begin'*. Make masks for the dance and music to accompany the movement. Create large monster paintings. Ask: *What are the monsters and why does Max send them to bed? What do you think his parents are like?*

The Elephant and the Bad Baby

Elfrida Vipont and Raymond Briggs (Puffin)

This wonderful cumulative tale has been around for almost 50 years. Enjoy the story with everyone joining in. Ask: *Is the baby really a 'bad' baby?* Draw long maps so that the children can see the story pattern. Act the story out for an assembly. Retell the tale, visiting different places (perhaps local to you) and with different characters. Ask: *What other book has a similar ending where they all go home for tea? (Mr Gumpy)*.

Avocado Baby

John Burningham (Bloomsbury)

Of course, start with a discussion about babies – and bring in an avocado for tasting (marvel at the huge seed and plant it). Enjoy the ridiculous humour (the Popeye theme) and talk about being strong and weak. Ask: *What do you think the baby will do next?* Watch the bullies get their come-uppance! Create new stories based on the same idea featuring babies that will only eat one food and gain a superpower, such as a 'Banana Baby' that can fly!

The Tiger Who Came to Tea

Judith Kerr (HarperCollins)

Role-play the scene where Daddy returns and they tell him the story of what happened when the tiger came to tea. Ask: *What can you spot in the scene in which the family is walking to the café?* (A cat appears that looks like the tiger.) Apparently, the tiger never came again – but retell the story of when a different animal came to tea! Create a collage of an enormous tiger.

Lost and Found

Oliver Jeffers (HarperCollins)

Tell the children some things about penguins… and about a 'lost and found office'. Then, read and enjoy this strange tale. Ask: *What interests you in the tale? Why does the penguin follow the boy?* Role play the scene in which they go to the office. Ask: *What is 'disappointment'?* Tell stories to the penguin – make a boat in the class and provide a cuddly penguin to tell stories to and *'talk about wonderful things'*. Ask: *Why is the penguin sad when they reach the South Pole? What was the 'big mistake'?*

Knuffle Bunny

Mo Willems (Hyperion Books)

Yet another story about loss, but this time it is the loss of a cuddly bunny and not a mother (*Dogger* has a similar plot). The key to the story involves knowing what an 'errand' and a 'Laundromat' might be! The inside title page provides some interesting background detail worth discussing. Discuss the moment of realisation. Ask: *Why doesn't Dad understand and what advice would you give him? Why is it that Mum understands immediately?* Practise going 'boneless' and showing Trixie's emotions with just your faces! Collect baby, family or made-up class words. Ask: *How do you think the images were created?* (Ink sketches and digital photography.) Try the same technique!

Beegu
Alexis Deacon (Random House)

Read slowly and give time for children's spontaneous comments. Re-read and track the ups and downs of what happens and what Beegu feels and might be thinking. Role play conversations between the characters that Beegu meets and a new character, explaining what happened. Role play conversations between Beegu's parents. Write letters from Beegu to the children and from the children to Beegu. Ask: *What would Beegu want to know or be interested in?* Create small worlds or larger areas into which a Beegu/ET character arrives and tries to make friends.

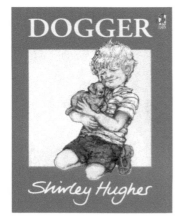

Dogger
Shirley Hughes (Random House)

This is a classic and necessary picture book for infants. It is about sacrifice or giving things up for other people to make them feel OK – though the moral doesn't need spelling out as the children will instinctively understand this truth. Obviously, this does however call for a big talk about special cuddly toys, mementoes and objects. Bring in your own cuddly toy! Track and discuss the ups and downs of the characters – Bella, Dave, Mum and Dad and of course the little girl. Everyone is feeling different! Ask: *What would you say to Bella?* Write a thank you letter from Dave to Bella.

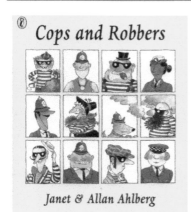

Cops and Robbers
Alan and Janet Ahlberg (Puffin)

Draw the street map that appears in the book. Collect a box of the missing toys. Read in conjunction with *Burglar Bill* (Puffin). Read and chant together the story many times. You will need many copies of the book for the children to spot and talk about all the details in the drawings. Quite a lot of vocabulary will need discussing – from crowbars to truncheons! Create huge WANTED posters. Get a plastic helmet for play and for reading the story in role as Officer Pugh!

Elmer
David McKee (Andersen Press)

After reading the book ask the children: *What is the best thing about Elmer? Why is Elmer feeling worried? Were the animals really laughing because he was different? In what way was Elmer different? How do we feel different?* This book offers plenty to discuss. Draw the outline of large elephants and design a multi-coloured patchwork Elmer with tissue paper, felt, paint, crayons or different materials, using squares or triangles or rectangles or other patterns.

Pie Corbett's
Reading Spine

In Year 2, it is important to start to move from sharing picture books into sharing chapter books. These will not only provide a meaty read, but also demand that the children use their imagination. Of course, there are also many Reception and Year 1 children who will sit and enjoy a chapter book and this should form part of their reading experience. Many of the chosen books operate on different levels - from the satisfaction of good stories to the exploration of deeper themes.

Traction Man is Here   Picture books

Mini Grey (Random House)

With the class read the pictures carefully, looking for details. Discuss together any difficult words. Re-read a number of times and talk about how the characters feel. Bring into school other kitchen equipment and encourage children to invent further adventures for Traction Man and Scrubbing Brush. Ask: *Are the adventures real? Who made them up?* Design Traction Man adverts or invent a new superhero or heroine.

Meerkat Mail

Emily Gravett (Macmillan)

Begin by finding out a bit about meerkats and the other animals, such as jackals. Watch meerkats on film with the class. Invite the children to write a newspaper article about Sunny's visit to one of the places in the book. Encourage them to write postcards from other visits that he made. Together draw a map of the story. Also, read *Wolves* (Macmillan) and *Little Mouse's Big Book of Fears* (Macmillan).

Amazing Grace   READ&RESPOND

Mary Hoffman (Frances Lincoln)

With the class tell or read the stories mentioned: Joan of Arc, Anansi, The Wooden Horse, Hannibal, *Treasure Island*, Hiawatha, Mowgli, Aladdin and Dick Whittington. Ask: *What sort of person is Grace? Where are the clues? In the story, are Raj and Natalie right? Which is the most important line in the story?* (Possibly '*you can be anything*'.) (See the *Read & Respond* title for further ideas.)

Pumpkin Soup

Helen Cooper (Corgi)

Read and enjoy the images and story. Ask the children: *What causes the argument and who was right?* Discuss how Cat and Squirrel's feelings change. Ask: *When are they happiest and why?* In role as Duck, tell the story of what happened when you left the Pumpkin. Also, with the class set the story to music, perform and dance with costumes and chant or sing with a dramatic chorus.

Who's Afraid of the Big Bad Book?

Lauren Child (Orchard Books)

Before reading this book it is essential to know the stories of Goldilocks, Rapunzel, Dick Whittington and Cinderella – so start by retelling these stories or some of the wit will be lost! Having really discussed the book, encourage the children to try falling 'into a book' and becoming a character in a well-known fairy tale, but then alter what happens. Take photos, enlarge and copy these for the children. Then, ask the children to draw characters and objects onto the photos, using Lauren Child's collage technique.

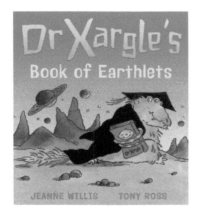

Dr Xargle's Book of Earthlets

Tony Ross (Andersen Press)

Read and enjoy – then discuss the funny bits. Ask: *What makes them amusing?* As a class collect some of the strange words that Dr Xargle uses and give them definitions, such as 'eggmangle', 'earthlet', 'hairdo of a sheep'. Ask: *What other strange things might aliens not understand if they came to earth?* Together make a little book of such misunderstandings.

Not Now Bernard

David McKee (Andersen Press)

Re-read a number of times and then discuss the parents, the child and the monster. Ask: *Who in the story is naughty? Are the parents ignoring the child or is he choosing the wrong moment? Are they too busy? Are they kind parents? What does the monster stand for? When do we feel or behave like monsters?* Let the children take it in turn to role play being Mum and Dad and talk about what has happened in the kitchen!

Tuesday

David Wiesner (Andersen Press)

After reading ask the children: *What do the frogs remind you of on the leaves?* (Flying saucers.) Hot-seat the man at 11.21pm. Ask: *Why do the frogs fall off the leaves? Why is the last frog looking grumpy?* Then turn the opening pages into a story. As the detective, encourage the children to interview the man in pyjamas and write up a police report. Together role play the news report and make a film of the interview and news item. Ask: *What happens the next Tuesday at 7.58pm?*

The Flower

John Light (Child's Play)

Before reading ask the class: *From the cover what might the book be about? How do the city people feel at the start of the book?* Pause on the page in the library and see what the children notice. Ask: *Why might books be dangerous? Why might a book be labelled 'do not read'?* Discuss the two books mentioned in the border: 'Jack and the Beanstalk' and *Alice in Wonderland*. Ask: *What do they have in common and how do they differ? Why were they chosen?* Stop where Brigg is reading the book and discuss what the book is about. Ask: *Why does he read it in secret?* Then read straight through and discuss the theme again at the end of the book.

Gorilla   READ&RESPOND

Anthony Browne (Walker Books)

Read through the story and discuss. Re-read and look more carefully at the pictures. With the class make a list of strange things. Discuss the Dad and the Girl. Ask: *What do they want?* Talk about their relationship. Ask: *Who is the gorilla? If you had to say what the book was about in one word, what word would you choose? Which is the most important picture and why?* (See *Read & Respond* title for further ideas.)

Emily Brown and The Thing

Cressida Cowell (Orchard Books)

I would start this by bringing in a 'cuddly' and discussing why they are so important! Also, provide other 'Emily Brown' books for free reading, including *That Rabbit Belongs to Emily Brown* (Orchard Books). On the first reading, stop on the page where Emily asks, *What's really the matter?* and predict. Re-read and discuss the challenging vocabulary – provide pictures and relate words to children's own experiences, listing synonyms. Tell a story that Emily might have told the witches and discuss the use of the font changes. Discuss what the story is about – especially the end. With the class make lists of nice/scary things and write as list poems.

Frog and Toad Together Novels

Arnold Lobel (HarperCollins)

Each of the five stories is a little gem. Here are some simple ideas for each tale:

1. Prepare model making lists with the class of what needs to be done and have children make 'job lists'.
2. Grow seeds: choose stories, poems, songs and play music for the seeds.
3. Bake cookies and discuss the need for 'will power'.
4. List brave characters for stories and discuss what it means to be brave.
5. What does the dream story mean?

Finally, ask: *What do the stories tell us about the different characters of Frog and Toad?* Read through and list clues. Ask: Why would they make good friends? Which is your favourite story and why? Also, read *Frog and Toad are Friends* (HarperCollins).

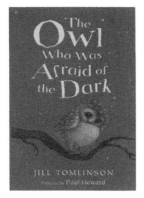

The Owl Who Was Afraid of the Dark READ&RESPOND

Jill Tomlinson (Puffin)

List and discuss fears about the dark saying: *you are only afraid of the dark because you don't know about it.* Role play Plop talking with the different characters. Write a letter to Plop to persuade him that the dark is actually friendly. Use an image of an owl (or the real thing if available) and draw in your 'nature sketch book'. Ask: *How has Plop changed by the end?* Write list poems about the dark. Find out about other nocturnal animals and create constellations. Paint and create owl collages and masks. Revisit *Owl Babies* (Walker Books). (See the *Read & Respond* title for further ideas.)

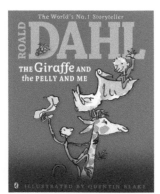

The Giraffe, the Pelly and Me

Roald Dahl (Puffin)

This is a meaty read. Begin by finding out a bit about giraffes, pelicans and monkeys. Invite the class to write adverts for 'The Ladderless Window Cleaning Company' and invent names for new sweets. Discuss the final song and its meaning. Draw 'The Grubber'. Ask: *What dreams would you have?* Learn, sing (or chant) and perform the various songs with the class. (See the *Read & Respond* title for further ideas.)

Fantastic Mr Fox READ&RESPOND

Roald Dahl (Penguin)

Before reading, it might be worth finding out a little about foxes. Draw the three farmers and collect information/quotes about them from the book. Re-read and savour the great writing in Chapter 3. Invite children to write letters to the farmers from the crowd at the end of chapter 7. Before reading Chapter 9 ask: *What do you think Mr Fox's plan will be?* Pause in Chapter 12 and ask: *Are the other animals right?* Pause in Chapter 14 and ask: *Is stealing right in this case?* Discuss with the children whether farmers should shoot foxes. Then with the class role play the conversation between the farmers at the end. (See the *Read & Respond* title for further ideas.)

The Hodgeheg   READ&RESPOND

Dick King-Smith (Puffin)

Introduce the book by showing film/images of hedgehogs and discussing the problem they have with roads! Make a list of rules about crossing the road for Max. Ask: *What advice would you give Max about crossing the road?* Write sentences that swap over words and letters. Role play a family discussion about Max's condition in Chapter 4. Hot-seat the hedgehog Max meets in Chapter 5. Tell the story of 'the first crossing' and hot-seat the lollipop lady at the end! Next, try reading Dick King-Smith's *Fox Busters* (Puffin). (See the *Read & Respond* title for further ideas.)

Flat Stanley   READ&RESPOND

Jeff Brown (HarperCollins)

With the class use 'role on the wall' to collect insights into the family and ask: *What are they like and how do we know?* Together explore their feelings and list the advantages of being flat. Encourage the children to write the police report for Chapter 2 and the invite from Thomas. As journalists, invite them to interview Stanley and write a news report for Chapter 4. Discuss the teasing in Chapter 5 and how the boys feel. Finally, can they write another adventure for Stanley? Make available the other 'Flat Stanley' books for independent or guided reading. (See the *Read & Respond* title for further ideas.)

Willa and old Miss Annie

Berlie Doherty (Catnip)

This is a gentle, deep book of three linked stories that should be savoured and thought about.

1. Read pages 1 and 2: discuss what will happen, who is Joshua and how will they all become friends. Read 5 pages and ask: *Who is lost? What is 'Joshua' about in one word?*
2. In 'The Bony' discuss the rights and wrongs. Ask: *What would you say to Silas and Molly?*
3. Discuss pets and friends. Ask: *Can wild animals be pets?*

Pie Corbett's
Reading Spine

Whilst I have selected just one picture book for Year 3, there are many more which will intrigue and provide a challenge for this age group such as The Day the Crayons Quit (HarperCollins) or John Brown, Rose and the Midnight Cat (Puffin). Children of this age need a great storyline, but should also be experiencing deep and rich books.

The Iron Man `READ & RESPOND`

Ted Hughes (Faber)

Notice and imitate the opening, using rhetorical questions to draw in the reader. With the class role play the family talking about the picnic or Hogarth telling his parents about what he had seen. Invite them to create a diary for Hogarth and news bulletins for both the Iron Man and space-bat-angel-dragon. Discuss which of the two tales is strongest and why? Ask them to draw parallels with other 'taming the monster' stories. (See the *Read & Respond* title for further ideas.)

Cat Tales: Ice Cat

Linda Newberry (Usborne)

With the class look at the use of imagery on the first few pages and make a list of other similes for snow. Ask: *What else is white? Why does Tom feel funny about Gary's dad in Chapter 1? How can a creature be in the snow? Why does Tom feel bad-tempered with his dad in Chapter 2?* Talk about the lump of ice inside of him. Ask: *In Chapter 3 what is the Ice Cat searching for? In Chapter 4 how can the cat's touch be inside of Tom and why does he destroy the snowman and blame the Ice Cat?* In Chapter 5 explain the Ice Green Cat's role in the story and why the icy hardness melts away. Ask: *What is it all about?*

The Sheep-pig `READ & RESPOND`

Dick King-Smith (Puffin)

Remind the children that they have previously read a Dick King-Smith novel, *Hodgeheg* (Puffin). Not surprisingly, he used to be a farmer. Ask: *Are pigs stupid?* (See Chapter 2.) *Why does Fly look after Babe? At the start of Chapter 3 what are the puppies not telling Babe?* Discuss the relationship between Fly and Babe. Ask: *What is it about Babe's character that is so endearing?* Invite the children to write the police report about the sheep rustling incident and the news report about the sheep-dog trials. (See the *Read & Respond* title for further ideas.)

The Abominables

Eva Ibbotson (Scholastic)

This is a longer read. To set the scene, begin with some introduction to the Abominable Snowman, the Yeti and the mountains of Tibet. Together predict what might happen from the first sentence. After reading Chapter 2 ask them to write stories to read to the yetis. Ask: *How is 'the world outside changing' and why is this an issue?* After reading Chapter 3 can they write a newspaper story about the yetis? After reading Chapter 5 discuss whether the plan is a good one. After reading Chapter 13 encourage the class to write a leaflet to persuade people to help the yetis. As a final task, together rename the story! Also, read *Journey to the River Sea* (Macmillan) and *One Dog and his Boy* (Marion Lloyd Books).

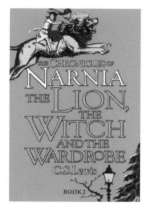

The Lion, the Witch and the Wardrobe   READ & RESPOND

CS Lewis (HarperCollins)

After reading, ask the class to write list poems '*through the magic door/ I saw…*'. Re-read and discuss together the reaction of the Professor. Draw the lantern in the snow with the trees and ask them to write a description. In small groups recreate the meal in Mr Tumnus's house and describe it. Discuss together which is the key scene and what it means. Draw a Narnia map and invite children to draw in episodes. Encourage the children to write information reports about some of the magical creatures and design traps for the nasty ones! Together make character charts for each character to compare and contrast. With permission watch the film in lesson. Then use role play to explore conversations between the children about Edmund's behaviour. Explain his actions. Ask: *Why is he forgiven?* (See the *Read & Respond* title for further ideas.)

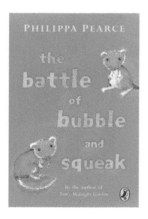

The Battle of Bubble and Squeak

Philippa Pearce (Penguin)

With the class create role-on-the-wall for Sid, Bill and Alice Sparrow. Ask: *How does the writer show their characters?* Use diary entries or hot-seating to keep alive the different viewpoints of what is happening in the family. Pause at the end of Chapter 10 asking them to predict how it might end. Discuss the end of the story. Interestingly, the story is based on two gerbils that Philippa Pearce's daughter Sally kept, as she said: "*almost all the incidents… happened to us: [the gerbils] gnawed holes in the curtains, the cat caught one and we had to take it to the vet. Our gerbil never fully recovered, but happily the fictional one does.*"

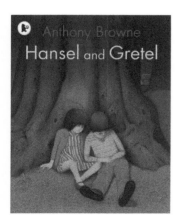

Hansel and Gretel   Picture book

Anthony Browne (Walker Books)

Read a version of the original and compare it together with the class. Read the story without showing the pictures to the children, then read with the pictures. Spend time looking at each picture, so the children can notice the visual play and discuss the changes in mood the artist portrays. Encourage them to imagine being in the wood and ask: *What would you see, hear, feel, think?* Then create list poems from these ideas. Discuss the step-mother/witch and the visual imagery. Ask: *Are they just tricks? What should the father have done?* Discuss the role of poverty in the story.

Pie Corbett's
Reading Spine

This selection covers a range of stories that extends to fantasy as well as introducing Anne Fine's wonderful books. I came across Perry Angel's Suitcase by Glenda Millard in Australia. It is a deeply moving book, both sad, but also full of hope – a lovely book. Read it yourself before reading it with the children to judge whether it is right for your class.

Bill's New Frock READ&RESPOND

Anne Fine (Egmont)

Read the first sentence and then discuss how might things be different for Bill. With the class list and discuss the various things that happen to Bill as a girl. The book was written in 1989, so together consider if anything has changed since then. Act out the classroom scene in Chapter 2. Discuss the line *'I am a person'* in Chapter 7. Encourage the children to write an extra scene for the book. (See the *Read & Respond* title for further ideas.)

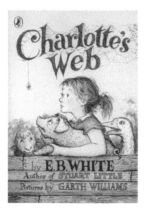

Charlotte's Web READ&RESPOND

EB White (Puffin)

It is 63 years on, but it is still a great read, starting with such a startling opening: *"Where's Papa going with that axe?"* With the class track the different characters, gathering clues about their different natures. Also, chart with a character graph how Wilbur's character develops. Produce a class timeline to show the sequence of events, so the plot can be seen in one glance. Role play conversations between Fern and Avery about different events, revisiting what has happened and discuss the implications of the key events. (See the *Read & Respond* title for further ideas.)

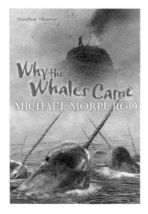

Why the Whales Came READ&RESPOND

Michael Morpurgo (Egmont)

Provide the children with some information about Narwhals as they feature in the story. Also, check out Bryher on the Isles of Scilly, and Rushy Bay – which is a key setting – and research on the internet why families left Samson Island. On the board draw a map of Bryher and together label with events. Ask: *How do our views of the Birdman change and why?* Issues to discuss in class: fear, bullying, friendship and should whales be hunted. (See the *Read & Respond* series for further ideas.)

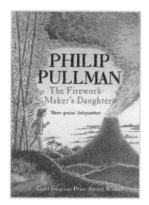

The Firework-Maker's Daughter

Phillip Pullman (Random House)

As a class invent names for new fireworks and draw designs for amazing explosive fireworks! Encourage children to write a letter from Lachand back to Lila (Chapter 2). Ask: *What is the big challenge that Lila faces?* Then in groups they can act out the scene where Lila meets Razvani. ask: *How does the author show how Lila feels in Chapter 5?* 'Illusions': *what does this mean in Chapter 5? What sort of person is Lila?* Invite them to gather evidence. Provide time to create persuasive adverts for a firework show by Lila and Lachand. Also, read *The Scarecrow and his Servant* (Random House) by the same author.

The Snow Walker's Son

Catherine Fisher (Red Fox)

From a 'Fire' daughter to a 'Snow' son, this is the first part of a powerful trilogy involving *'magic'* written by the Welsh novelist and poet, Catherine Fisher. Track the two main characters, Kari and Jessa, perhaps using a class timeline to show the main events and their developing characters. With the class make notes and discuss at the end the role of heat and cold in the story. Can they predict (or write) what might happen in the next story, The Empty Hand (Red Fox)?

Perry Angel's Suitcase

Glenda Millard (Phoenix Yard Books)

Read this book yourself before sharing it with the class. Discuss in lesson how everyone feels before Perry arrives and then discuss Perry's behaviour, thinking about why he acts as he does. Discuss the suitcase. Pause in Chapter 10 to discuss why Perry gets onto the raft. Ask: *What advice can be learned from Chapter 10?* Discuss the viewpoints of those involved at the end of each chapter. The themes run deep and it will help for children to talk about their feelings. There are other books in this series, all equally magical.

Voices in the Park `Picture book`

Anthony Browne (Random House)

Read the book through several times. Ask the children to list 'things to talk about' or 'questions' then discuss. Ask: *How do you feel about each character and why? (Is the mother really a bad mother? Where is the dad? Why does she wear a bowler hat? Is it right that the girl makes the dad a cup of tea?)* Together place them in order of sympathy. Then discuss relationships. Ask: *Which is the most important picture? Why? How long did the story take to read? What is the story about? What is its theme?* Discuss the pictures, use of colour, playfulness, lines and the font used. Also, study *The Tunnel* (Walker Books) by the same author.

Pie Corbett's
Reading Spine

It was only when I had made my list for Year 5 that I realised how animals feature heavily – cats, wolves and foxes! These are romping reads as well as stories that touch deeply. I have listed them in a suggested order that leads towards what I would say is the greatest novel ever written for children.

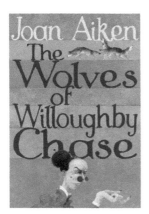

The Wolves of Willoughby Chase

Joan Aiken (Red Fox)

There are 12 novels in this series (the 'Wolves Chronicles') and 'The Wolves' is the first, set in Joan Aiken's own historical world (1832) where wolves have travelled through the Channel Tunnel! Begin by researching some information about wolves. There is a good film that can be used to compare with the book (though it has a PG certificate so get parental permission). Try reading the book chapter-by-chapter and watching the film alongside, section-by-section. With the class list difficult vocabulary for discussion and create a glossary of historical terms. At the end, discuss what should happen to Miss Slighcarp and Mr Grimshaw. Check out Joan Aiken's website where you can download a bookmark for the book. (http://www.joanaiken.com/pages/books.html)

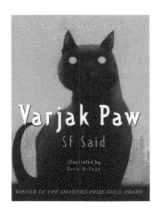

Varjak Paw   READ&RESPOND

SF Said (Random House)

After reading the book, ask children to paint dark city landscapes and skylines. Then together draw role-on-the-wall for Varjak, collecting clues and quotes about his developing character. Ask: *Why is Varjak rejected and yet why does he return?* Explain the difference between Varjak, the Elder Paw and the other cats. Can the children contrast the inside of the house with outside in the city? Together invent a 'Jalal tale' and explain 'the way'. Invite the children to write a night adventure for Varjak – for example, a story in which he nearly gets caught by Sally Bones. Encourage them to write a sequel adventure and then read *The Outlaw Varjak Paw* (Random House).

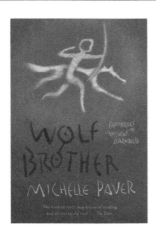

Wolf Brother

Michelle Paver (Orion)

Before reading draw a map and during the story, mark where events occur. With the class make a list of the words or phrases that Wolf uses instead of human terms and give their definitions, such as *'Tall Tailless, Bright White Eye, thundering Wet'*. Encourage them to try inventing other phrases for everyday things and try writing a scene from the book from Wolf's viewpoint using his language. The story is set 6,000 years ago and imagines what life might have been like. Together describe the main settings – the Raven camp, the ice river, the wide water, the cave and the forest. Draw and discuss as a class the significance of the main events – Torak's father's death, meeting Wolf, fighting Hord, discovering the prophecy and defeating the bear. Compare this book to other 'quests' – typical characters, events and plot patterns.

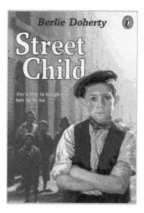

Street Child   READ&RESPOND

Berlie Doherty (HarperCollins)

Based on the true story of an orphan, Jim Jarvis, who inspired Dr Barnardo to set up his famous children's home, this book is ideal as a read for any Victorian project. Background work on Barnardo and the life of street children would set the context. Read *'Tell me your story Jim'* and in pairs invent a possible tale for Jim. In role as 'agony aunts' ask children to advise Jim after each chapter on his next moves. Map the story as it unfolds and at the end have them retell Jim's story in role as they now know it. At the end, discuss *'what is a home?'*, children's rights and how Jim survived. (See the *Read & Respond* title for further ideas.)

The Midnight Fox   READ&RESPOND

Betsy Byars (Faber)

Read the first two paragraphs and discuss as a class what the story might be about. Tom says: *'I like the way I am'*. Discuss the tension between his father's and Uncle Fred's expectations and Tom's view. Ask the children to invent newspaper titles for key incidents and use these to label a class map of the story. Provide time to write letters to Petie Burkis about the main events. Ask: *Why did Uncle Fred and Aunt Millie 'never mention what I had done'?* At the end, Tom says *'it was as if it had happened to another boy'*. What did happen? How did he change? Then discuss who was right: Uncle Fred or Tom?

Tom's Midnight Garden   READ&RESPOND

Philippa Pearce (Oxford University Press)

This book demands a timeline of events so that the class can see the way in which the plot is constructed and how time shifts. (You can see the house that Philippa Pearce used as a basis for the book online: http://www.dailymail.co.uk/news/article-2644779/Country-house-inspired-Philippa-Pearces-Toms-Midnight-Garden-goes-market-3-5million.html) Mime moving as a ghost through a door into a different world. When reading Chapter 20 discuss *'time no longer'*. Before reading Chapter 26, discuss with the class how the tale will end. Invite them to draw the garden and write an extra episode for Tom and Hatty. Can they write their own midnight trip into another world, such as *Pie's Midnight Forest* and identify the link with time travel in *The Lion, The Witch and the Wardrobe* from Year 3? (See the *Read & Respond* title for further ideas.)

FArTHER   Picture book

Grahame Baker-Smith (Templar)

Begin by reading the cover and ask: *Why is the title 'FArTHER'? Why the poppies? The birds? The wings? Are dreams important?* Explain *'another call claimed him'*. Ask: *What is the story about? What does it mean to each child?* Gather clues as a class about each character and then interview them in turn – mother, father and son. Also, read and explore the wonderful *Leon and the Place Between* (Templar), as well as picture books by David Wiesner, such as *Free Fall, Flotsam, Hurricane, Art and Max, June 29, 1999* and *Sector 7* (Houghton Mifflin).

Pie Corbett's
Reading Spine

Here is my selection of great novels for Year 6 children. Do also look out for Doris Lessing's Through the Tunnel (HarperCollins), which is a fabulous and challenging short story. These books are the reading rites of passage that pave the way for the great literature that lies ahead. The books are intense reads, meaty books that are crafted beautifully. They will stay with the reader forever. These books are life-changers. Do read them before sharing with the class as some touch on challenging themes.

Holes READ & RESPOND

Louis Sachar (Bloomsbury)

Invite the children to keep a diary for each of the key events – and by contrast, write a letter home from the camp. Together collect information about the main characters and discuss why they behave as they do. Ask: *Why did the author give Stanley a palindromic name?* Draw two timelines to track the present and past events. In role as journalists, encourage children to carry out interviews and write a news item for the start and end of the book. Ask: *Why is the book called 'Holes'?* Talk through all the possibilities. Discuss *'the holes in their lives'*. Then make a comparison with the film (it has a PG certificate, so you might want to check with parents before showing it). (See the *Read & Respond* title for further ideas.)

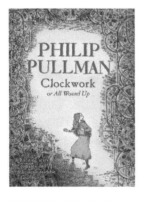

Clockwork

Philip Pullman (Random House)

Before reading, ask: *What does the cover suggest the book will be about?* While reading it in class create a story map of the story and show how the main events and characters interconnect. Ask: *Which are the good/bad characters? Where is your evidence?* Together compare Karl and Gretl using evidence from the text. Ask: *In what way is the book like 'clockwork'? How are our lives like clockwork? In what ways do we 'wind up the future like clockwork'?* Re-read the book and pause at the places where there is the most suspense. Ask: *How does Philip Pullman create suspense? What techniques does he use? How does he keep the reader 'all wound up'?*

The Hobbit

JRR Tolkein (HarperCollins)

With the class create maps and a timeline for the adventure. Can they write messages in runic code? Invite them to write letters to Bilbo to persuade him to join the journey. Together create a set of instructions, such as 'How to Trap a Troll'. Role play the Troll scene in lesson. Invite them to write riddles for Bilbo to use against Gollum or the Dragon. Provide time to write Gollum's story, asking: *How did he get inside the mountain and how did he come by the ring?* Together write a poem listing what you would do with a magical ring. After each key part of the story, interview a child in the role of a dwarf and ask them about what has happened or create and film news bulletins. Challenge children to draw or describe Smaug, as well as write an 'end of term report' for Bilbo. Ask: *How has the journey changed him?* Work out the underlying pattern of the Quest story – and the key archetypal characters – then create your own quest in chapters.

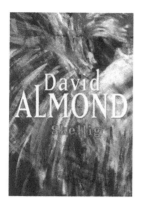

Skellig   READ&RESPOND

David Almond (Hodder)

Together in class discuss Mina's views on education. Ask: *Who or what is Skellig? What is the book about? Invite them to c*ollect key lines to talk about, such as *'truth and dreams are always getting muddled'*. In role as Mina, encourage children to write her diary extracts about what is happening. Perform and talk about 'Tyger' by William Blake. Provide time to write Michael's story for Miss Clarts in Chapter 33. Ask: *Why does Michael want to call the baby 'Persephone'?* Tell the class to read 'Mina – my story' and write a sequel to *Skellig*. (See the *Read & Respond* series for further ideas.)

Fireweed

Jill Paton Walsh (Hot Key Books)

This book benefits from background knowledge about the bombing of London in 1940 and the evacuation. Split the class in two with both halves keeping diary entries for the two main characters. Hold discussions after each chapter as this is a demanding read. Pause for 'think alouds' where children in role think aloud about their thoughts, hopes, motives, and so on. Discuss with the class what happens in the last two chapters. Ask: *Why is the story called 'Fireweed'?* Also, read *Dolphin Crossing* (Faber) by the same author (about Dunkirk).

River Boy

Tim Bowler (Oxford University Press)

This is another mysterious book and you should read it before reading it to the class. Ask: *Who, or what, is the 'river boy' and how can he be 'part of her'? What does Grandpa want? How can Jess 'be his hands'?* When reading Chapter 17 discuss the relationship between the painting and the river boy and Grandpa. Discuss the importance of the swim and ask: *how does this help Jess come to terms with Grandpa's death? By the end of the book who has changed and how?* At the end of the book discuss *the spirit of the river boy was in her alone*. Try to summarise what the book is about and what it means to the children. Some of these meanings might be private.

The Arrival   Picture book

Shaun Tan (Hodder)

Before reading this in class you may find it handy to explain immigration, especially the migration to America at the end of the 19th century (Ellis Island). Read carefully and discuss. Study each section at a time. Ask: *What is happening?* As there are no words, the reader has to work hard! Discuss in class how the story makes you feel – and how the characters seem to feel. (Being in a new country, migrants often feel at a loss in the same way that the reader does.) Discuss the three 'helpers'. Invite the children to write the letters that they send. Ask: *What is the story about? Are all the illustrations real or in someone's imagination? Are they symbols for anything?* Encourage the class to write story sections to go with different parts of the book or diary entries for characters. Also, read other Shaun Tan books, such as *The Lost Thing*, *The Red Tree* and *Rules of Summer* which makes a good model for writing. Also, check out picture books by Armin Greder, *The Island* and *The City* (Allen & Unwin).

Planning and preparing
your Reading Spine

Different stories require different responses and exploration, so it is important to think carefully about what lies at the heart of each story and how to deepen children's understanding and appreciation of it. Keep a wary eye on the need to make reading a rich and pleasurable experience. Ideally, you need enough books so that the children can share at least one copy between two.

Always read each book through yourself, and decide what to focus upon and how this can be achieved. Think about the particular demands and challenges of the book. *At what point will you need to stop and with which activity?* Of course, teachers should read aloud expressively, re-reading key passages and savouring beautiful language.

Tackle difficult vocabulary in various ways. For instance, you might help children understand words by showing an object, toy, picture or film. Some words are better understood by listing examples or by acting something out. Make lists of similar words or opposites and try the word in other sentences. Sometimes reading on, or re-reading, will provide clues to a word's meaning. The most powerful strategy is to try and relate the tricky word to the children's own experience. Get them to explain the word to their partner, display the word and rehearse using it in sentences over a number of days to add it to their repertoire.

Agree on your 'Rules for Book Discussions'	Collect 'ways to talk about books'
All ideas are accepted	*It reminds me of …*
Everyone should 'have a go'	*I'm not sure but…*
Be ready to change your mind	*We wondered whether…*
Listen to each other	*I like that idea but…*
It helps to be tentative, e.g. *'we wondered whether…'*	*It is the same as …*
	It appears to be …
You can	*We think that …*
a. Suggest new ideas	*The writer suggests that …*
b. 'Build' on someone's ideas	*Perhaps, …*
c. Explain your ideas	*It makes me think of …*
d. Ask questions	*The main point might be …*

Planning to use a picture book
with children aged 3-7

Reread a picture book over a number of days – for pleasure, primarily. However, deepen understanding and appreciation by working closely with a well-loved book. You might take a different focus for each rereading. Different books lend themselves to different approaches - for example:

DAY 1	DAY 2
Discuss your expectation of the content from the cover/title then read the book through, for the pleasure of a great story. Focus on prediction, with occasional pauses to discuss what might happen next. After reading, take initial reactions to the story – ask children to discuss their preferences, anything that concerned them (raising questions and 'wondering') and possible links to their own lives. Focus on the story in the pictures compared to the story in the words.	Reread the book, encouraging children to 'join in'. Point to words as you read them. Focus on 'vocabulary', i.e. which words or phrases need to be discussed so that the children understand what the words mean. Teach vocabulary by thinking of similar words/ opposites, use props or images, mime words, relate to children's experiences, put the words into other sentences, explain meanings. Try using sticky notes to change words and discuss how this alters meaning.
DAY 3	**DAY 4**
Reread with children increasingly joining in and the teacher withdrawing. Focus on 'sentences': discussing, trimming, imitating, altering as well as punctuation. Try saying sentences in different ways in relation to their meaning – loud, soft, quick, slow, with differing expressions. Read with expression: contrast by reading in a dull voice. Discuss 'how it should sound'.	Ask the children to reread more fluently. Focus on character: *how does the character feel? What might they be thinking? How do we know?* Discuss the story from different viewpoints. Use drama to bring scenes alive, e.g. hot seat, freeze frame, phone call, role-play. Focus on inference – what is suggested but not written.

❝ Focus on the story in the pictures compared to the story in the words. ❞

DAY 5

Ask the children to reread. Make links with other books. What is the main idea, message or theme? Find key images, words or parts of the story. Look at the underlying pattern. Story map the book and ask them to retell in their own words

Planning to use a novel
with children aged 7-11

Think about whether you need to do any activities **BEFORE** you start the novel, to tune the children into the context. Then plan what activities do you need to do **DURING** the story and what you will do **AFTER**. Each novel will demand different activities or moments for discussion.

Activities Before Reading

Do we need to develop the context so that the story makes more sense? E.g. reading *Fireweed* is enriched by knowing something about the Blitz and evacuees.
Explore 'expectations': what is the book about from the title, cover or chapter headings?

Activities During Reading

a. Picture it: activities to help us 'imagine'

- draw scenes and rewrite a section from the imagination
- draw and label a scene
- respond to illustrations and describe
- track a plot by creating a timeline, story board or map
- display a story museum of objects and costumes from the story
- draw a 'role on the wall' with character quotes and clues
- use costumes, props and devise artefacts for the story, e.g. a letter, message, map mentioned in the text.

b. Live it: activities that help us become part of the story

- create story artefacts, e.g. a message/email arrives or an object is found
- drama (phone calls, hot seat, news reports, role-play, freeze frame, agony aunt, etc.)
- write in role (letters, diaries, news items, etc.)
- create a blog for the main character or a character tweets
- internalise language through children preparing group performances of key sections.

c. Understand it: activities to deepen our appreciation

- hold 'book discussions' at key moments
- predict the next events, connect and tie up clues across a section
- create character profiles or graphs, using quotes and clues
- focus on the author's style through cloze procedure.

Activities After Reading

- rewrite the story as a mini story of 150 words
- write a character's end of year school 'report'
- write and design the book 'blurb', front cover or advertise the story
- compare the 'start' to the 'end' and discuss 'changes'
- select the key line/ passage and discuss what the story is about.

Notes

Pie Corbett's Reading Spine

SCHOLASTIC

Build a read-aloud programme with great value book packs

Modern children's classics chosen by Pie Corbett – available in packs
for Nursery–Year 6, individually and in sets of 6 and 30

Nursery Pack (12 books)*
£79.00 £63.90*
SY5990

Reception Pack (12 books)*
£81.00 £65.50
SY6018

Year 1 Pack (12 books)*
£81.00 £65.50
SY6052

Year 2 Pack (18 books)*
£120.82 £96.66
SY6089

Year 3 Pack (7 books)*
£41.93 £33.54
SY6102

Year 4 Pack (7 books)*
£45.93 £36.74
SY6115

Year 5 Pack (7 books)*
£46.93 £37.54
SY6128

Watch Pie Corbett's
Reading Spine video at
www.scholastic.co.uk/piecorbett

Year 6 Pack (7 books)*
£52.93 £42.34
SY6144

Order your books now at www.scholastic.co.uk/piecorbett

*Selection of books from pack s...